STURMGESCHÜTZ III
in action

by Bruce Culver

illustrated by Don Greer

Allgemaines
Sturmabzeichen
(Assault Badge)

 squadron/signal publications

Late StuG III ausf G of the Panzer Lehr Division, 1945. This vehicle, camouflaged in Dark Yellow and Green Camouflage, has the rare late addition of concrete re-inforcement to the superstructure.

ISBN 0-89747-047-8

Also by Bruce Culver

Panther in Action
Pzkpfw IV in Action

with Bill Murphy
Panzer Colors

Photo Credits

Bundesarchiv, Koblenz
National Archives
Archives Publiques
U.S. Army

Distributed in Great Britain By
by Almark Publishing Co. Ltd.,

Three StuG III ausf B's seen in Russia, 1941. The first two vehicles have the wider 40 cm track and later drive sprockets; the third vehicle - to the left - has retained the original pattern sprockets. All these vehicles have the old rear idler and the repositioned front return roller. [Bundesarchiv]

StuG III Development

Within a year of the formation of the new Wehrmacht under Hitler's Third Reich, the requirements for the basic battle tanks and many of the tactics to be used had been accepted by the German High Command. Although the nascent panzer divisions had a secure future, many infantry officers were concerned about the lack of a vehicle suitable for supporting infantry advances. Many high ranking infantry officers had come to see the need for a heavily armored support gun that could eliminate strong points and obstacles during an assault; the experiences of World War I had also contributed to the demand for such a vehicle controlled by the infantry for best effect.

In 1936, the German High Command ordered the development of a suitable armored support vehicle, mounting the 7.5 cm L/24 howitzer then being adopted for the PzKpfw IV medium tank. Daimler-Benz had the responsibility for the design of the chassis and superstructure, and Krupp had the job of developing the gun and the new mounting.

In 1937, five "O"-series prototypes were built, using the modified chassis of the PzKpfw III ausf B. These five vehicles mounted the 7.5 cm howitzer in a low, fixed superstructure; the mount had limited traverse, suitable for fine corrections in aiming. Because these pilot models were constructed of mild steel, they were not to be used in combat, though service trials helped in developing the initial production version, the Sturmgeschütz III ausf A.

The ausf A's were assembled by Alkett in Berlin, and 4 batteries of these vehicles were in action from the beginning of the 1940 campaign against France and the Low Countries. The ausf B, C, D and E also mounted the L/24 howitzer in keeping with the vehicle's intended use as an infantry support weapon.

Events in Russia after the start of "Barbarossa" in June, 1941, proved to be traumatic for Germany's armor leaders. The T-34 and KV-1 were clearly superior to the standard German tanks, and only poor Russian tactics and superior German training and discipline salvaged the initial German advances. The StuG III in particular had proved effective as an improvised antitank weapon, largely because of its low shape and thicker frontal armor. Nonetheless, it was obvious that the L/24 howitzer was not an effective weapon against the T-34, much less the heavier KV-1. Hitler demanded a longer gun and the ausf F mounting a new 7.5 cm L/43 (later L/48) gun appeared in 1942.

With the introduction of the L/43 gun, the StuG III was more often used as an antitank weapon, once more leaving the infantry without a support vehicle. As a result, a new version was developed, mounting a 10.5 cm howitzer for greater effectiveness as a support vehicle. Except for the weapon, the "Sturmhaubitze 42" was identical to the standard StuG III.

The final model, the ausf G, appeared in early 1943 and production continued to the end of the war. Various improvements were made in equipment and details, and because of the lower costs and faster production flow, the StuG III became a very important defensive weapon, excelling in the antitank role on the Eastern Front. Zimmerit, side skirting, roof-mounted machine guns and other features were added during production, but the basic design proved to be effective and was well-liked by the crews. At least one

This front view of one of the 5 prototype vehicles shows the details that distinguish this first model. These units were built on the PzKpfw III ausf B chassis, and had mild steel superstructures. Though used for service trials and training, the lack of armor plate made them unsuitable for combat. The twin round access hatches in the nose indentify the "O" series vehicles from the front.

mockup was built for a new vehicle based on the PzKpfw III/StuG III chassis; this had a well-shaped superstructure almost identical to that of the "Hetzer," though somewhat larger. This did not reach production, and the standard StuG III and StuH 42 (ausf G) were made until the end.

The StuG III was an inexpensive and effective weapon. Though designed as a support vehicle, it saw its greatest use in the antitank role, where it served very well. By the spring of 1944, StuG III's were credited with the destruction of 20,000 Russian tanks, and many others were destroyed by the end of the war, and on other fronts. After the end of the war, StuG III's were used temporarily by several countries and they appeared in the Middle East during the Suez incident in 1956, having been supplied from stocks taken by the Russians after the war.

Though the StuG III ausf A seems to be vastly different from the later ausf G's, in fact there was a steady progression of improvements and development, each new model being based closely on the preceding type. The basic shape and size of the vehicle were set with the first model and subsequent versions differed only in details of shape and equipment. Later in the war, there was not time for the complete redesign that could have resulted in even more effective weapons, with the result that some prewar designs like the PzKpfw IV and StuG III soldiered on to the end of the war in forms very similar to the early models. Considering Germany's increasingly hopeless strategic position during the last year of the war, they served very well indeed.

StuG III ausf A (SdKfz 142)

After the first 5 prototypes of the "O" series had been constructed and tested, changes were made in the design of the vehicle, and a new chassis was selected. The "O" vehicles had been built on the chassis of the PzKpfw III ausf

StuG III ausf A

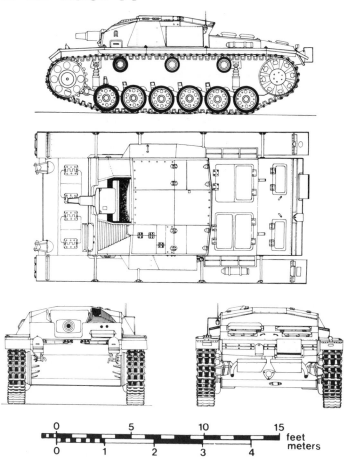

```
0          5          10          15
|----------|----------|----------|  feet
                                     meters
0      1      2      3      4
```

1:76 th scale (4 mm : 1 foot)

B, in itself a developmental design, and the production vehicles "Gepanzerte Selbstfahrlafette für Sturmgeschütz 7.5 cm Kanone ausf A, SdKfz 142" (later called StuG III ausf A) were based on the chassis of the PzKpfw III ausf F. The hulls were not tank components, being modified to suit the StuG III layout and having heavier armor, but the power train and suspension components were the same as those of the PzKpfw III ausf F (5/ZW).

The superstructure, bolted to the chassis with angles, was a low, relatively spacious fixed compartment with a multi-angled roof design and heavy frontal armor of 50 mm thickness. The chassis nose plates were also 50 mm thick as was the gun mantlet; there was another 50 mm plate behind the driver, at the forward end of the fighting compartment, and from the front, the StuG III ausf A was very well protected against the antitank guns of the period. The vertical side plates were 30 mm thick, the glacis plate was 26 mm, and the roof plates were 11 mm. On the left side was a rectangular armored pannier for the radio installation. In front of this box on the left, and all along the right side wall, an angled series of plates 9 mm thick formed an outer wall which extended over part of the mudguards. These angled plates were intended as extra spaced armor; nothing was stowed behind them, and there was no access to the space enclosed. The rear superstructure and rear hull plates were 30 mm thick, and the belly was 16 mm thick, with 20 mm lower nose and tail plates.

The gun was the standard 7.5 cm L/24 KwK 37 then being fitted to the PzKpfw IV medium tank, which was intended as a support vehicle for armored formations. Thus, since the StuG had not been intended to fight tanks or other moving targets, it did not need a turret, and the slightly smaller PzKpfw III chassis could mount the same gun. The mounting developed by Krupp was relatively primitive, consisting of a pedestal which was bolted to the floor, and with simple elevation and traverse mechanisms. No bullet splash protection was provided; this was particularly serious at maximum elevation. A canvas dust cover was provided to close the space around the mounting and protect the crew and equipment from dust and rain.

Access to the fighting compartment was through 3 hatches in the roof; in an emergency, the driver could escape through the inspection hatches in the glacis plate. The driver sat in front on the left; behind him was the gunner, and the commander occupied the left rear corner of the superstructure. The loader was at the right rear of the fighting compartment. The gunner's sight was internal, requiring a small aperture in the front plate, and a V-shaped cutout was made in the roof armor over the driver's compartment to allow a wider field of vision for the gunner. Metal ribs were welded in place to deflect ricocheting bullets and fragments.

The mechanical details were the same as the PzKpfw III ausf F. The suspension consisted of 6 pairs of roadwheels on each side, each set sprung by torsion bars and arms, with shock absorbers on the first and last axles. Because the torsion bars were paired, the wheels on the left were slightly behind those on the right side. Three return rollers were fitted, spaced equally. A built up, solid rear idler was used, and the cast drive sprocket had 8 lightening holes in the centers, driving 36 cm cast skeleton type tracks. The engine was a 12 cylinder Maybach HL120TR rated at 300 hp, and the transmission was the 10-speed preselective Variorex type. Steering was by clutch and brake.

Production began early in 1940, and 4 batteries of StuG III ausf A's saw service during the invasion of France in May, 1940. Additional units worked up to service status after the end of the campaign.

This high view of a StuG III ausf A shows the squat superstructure, front sighting aperture with the fan-shaped cutout in the driver's roof, and the extra stowage on the engine deck. A heavy cloud of dust obscures the chassis. This vehicle is from the 192nd Sturmgeschütz Abteilung.

Old Pattern Drive Sprocket

Old Pattern Rear Idler

A StuG III ausf A seen in Holland, 1940. Here can be seen the early chassis layout, based on the chassis of the PzKpfw III ausf F; note the early drive sprocket, rear idler, and roller spacing.

StuG III ausf B (SdKfz 142)

Improvements to the PzKpfw III were also introduced on the StuG III vehicles, and in the autumn of 1940, an improved model of the StuG III appeared. Designated ausf B, the new model had the same hull and superstructure as the ausf A, which can cause confusion in identifying these versions. The chassis mechanical details, however, were based on the PzKpfw III ausf H. The 10-speed Variorex preselective transmission was replaced by a ZF SSG77 6-speed transmission and a Maybach HL120TRM engine was fitted. Externally, very early ausf B's were identical to the ausf A. Shortly, however, a new chassis design was necessitated by the introduction of a new track, 40 cm wide. The forward return roller on each side was moved forward to support the track near the drive sprocket, and a new drive sprocket and rear idler were introduced. The rear idler was an open 8-spoke cast wheel, and the drive sprocket was also cast, having 6 openings in a somewhat dished wheel with a protruding hub. Due to the introduction of these features during the ausf B production run, some vehicles were fitted with old sprockets and new idlers, new sprockets and old idlers, or both old or new fittings. The old style sprockets could be adapted for the 40 cm track by adding a spacer ring to the assembly, as was done for some PzKpfw III's during this changeover period.

In all other respects, the ausf B was the same as the ausf A, and as production continued, additional StuG III units were formed. 1940 and early 1941 were spent in training exercises and development of tactics based on combat experiences in France.

Two crewmen load ammunition into this StuG III ausf B. The relocated front return roller can be seen. Note the extra track up front, and the original built up rear idler. The extra tracks not only provided some extra protection, but could also be used in field repairs for the vehicle's tracks. [Bundesarchiv]

This snow-camouflaged ausf B shows the altered front roller and later cast dished drive sprocket introduced with the 40 cm wide track.

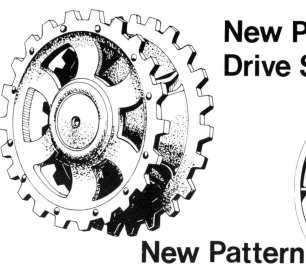

New Pattern Drive Sprocket

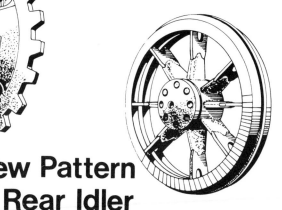

New Pattern Rear Idler

A useful high view of an ausf B, showing the stowage and rear hull details; note the railing that supports the spare track. [National Archives]

This ausf B, seen during the Russian winter, 1941-42, has a torn right mudguard, possibly the result of a mine explosion. The hinged slotted headlight cover allowed the headlight to be completely uncovered for driving in rear areas. Later the more effective Notek black-out lamp ["Tarnscheinwerfer"] was adopted. This vehicle also belongs to the 192nd Sturmgeschütz Abteilung. [Bundesarchiv]

Sturmgeschützbrigaden

 184. Sturmgeschützbrigade

 197. Sturmgeschützbrigade

 279. Sturmgeschützbrigade

 189. Sturmgeschützabteilung

 237. Sturmgeschützbrigade

 666. Sturmgeschützbatterie

 190. Sturmgeschützbrigade

 259. Sturmgeschützbrigade

 Sturmgeschützbrigade Großdeutschland

A light machine gun team rides a StuG III ausf B in Russia, 1941. The vehicle has the later drive sprocket, and the rear mudguards have been flipped up to keep mud from building up and fouling the track.

Both front mudguard flaps have been folded back on this ausf B, probably to prevent mud build-up, or damage from obstacles. Note the open sight aperture below the roof.

[Top Left] "BUSSARD", a StuG III ausf B, carries a well applied snow camouflage scheme. The canvas cover is black. Note the deflection of the front wheels as the vehicle hits a rise in the middle of this snow covered field. [Bundesarchiv]

Field maintenance was regular, if tedious, routine that all crews had to complete frequently to keep their vehicles ready for action. The men on the right are greasing the roadwheel bearings. The crewmen on the roof are probably working on the gun and sight. The heavy coating of mud on the suspension will probably be scraped off later, as this could cause problems if left on. [Bundesarchiv]

Changing a damaged drive sprocket was a three-man job. The white camouflage paint has been applied only to the upper superstructure. Patches of snow augment the painted snow effect. [Bundesarchiv]

Assault Gun Uniform, 1941

A StuG III ausf B carries infantry into the Ukraine during "Barbarossa." Note the two large beams carried to help in crossing antitank ditches and other obstacles. Again, the mudguards have been damaged, a very common condition. [Bundesarchiv]

StuG III ausf C & D (SdKfz 142)

In early 1941, a new model of the StuG III was introduced. This was the ausf C, and it differed from the ausf B in having a redesigned superstructure front. It had become obvious that the aperture for the gunner's sight compromised the front armor and a revised mounting for the sight was developed. With this design, the gunner's sight protruded through a slot in the roof plates. It traversed and elevated or depressed with the gun. Except for the slot, the roof design remained the same.

The front plates, however, were altered. The main 50 mm plate was now solid, and the side plates and driver's roof plates were also changed, resulting in a simpler, more effective shape. The front plates on the right side of the gun were changed the same way.

During production, several minor internal alterations were made, resulting in the model designation ausf D. There is no external difference between the two types, and the captions in this book will generally refer to these vehicles as ausf D's. From a number of angles, the ausf C and D resemble the ausf B, especially if the gunner's sight is hidden, so care must be taken in identifying these variants in photographs.

This front view of a new StuG III ausf C shows the redesigned superstructure which eliminated the front aperture for the gunner's sight; this was now mounted in the roof. The two holes over the driver's visor are for the driver's binocular vision device ["fahrerfernrohr"].

StuG III ausf C & D

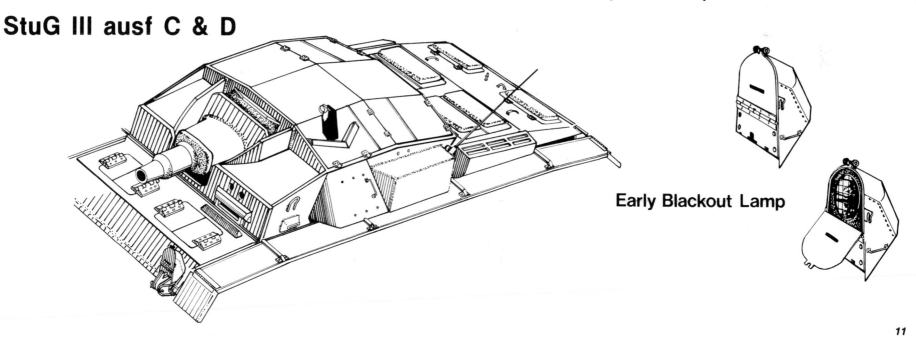

Early Blackout Lamp

11

A portable frame is used to lift the engine deck of this StuG III ausf D before engine maintenance. Work conditions in Russia were often very primitive, and much repair work was done outside. Spare track sections removed from the engine deck lie on the ground. [Bundesarchiv]

[Top Left] The revised superstructure front and roof-mounted gunner's sight are shown to good advantage here. Note the bullet splash rail protecting the sight. The commander is using the standard binocular artillery spotting telescope, here fitted with long sunshade tubes. The formed guards over the front lights are rather unusual. The chassis number [90630] identifies this StuG III as an ausf D. [Bundesarchiv]

This ausf D in the Crimean campaign in 1942 provides support for German infantry. The right mudguard was probably damaged by a mine; the suspension components were repaired to return the vehicle to service, but damaged sheet metal parts were usually removed and scrapped. [Bundesarchiv]

As a Russian village burns in the distance, crewmen replenish the ammunition stowage in this ausf D. Note the stowing arrangement for the spare track across the engine deck. Brackets with vertical rods are attached to the decking; the rods extend up through the holes in the guide teeth, holding the track in place. The trailer at the right was a standard design, used for several types of light and medium ammunition stores.

Binocular Sight

A StuG III ausf D passes a 3.7 cm PAK 36 and crew in Russia. The dark gray paint is covered with dust, and since the fixed superstructure did not require a clear engine deck, it was common for a large amount of stowage to be carried on top of the engine compartment.

StuG III
ausf C & D

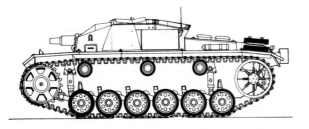

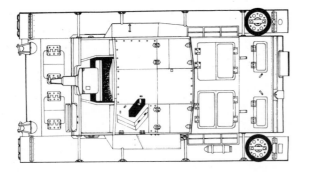

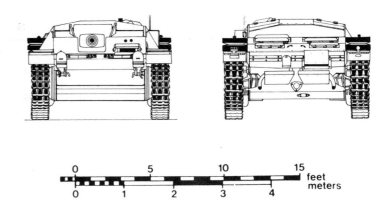

0 5 10 15 feet
meters
0 1 2 3 4

1:76 th scale (4 mm:1 foot)

A group of StuG III's in Russia in 1942. The vehicle on the right is an ausf E;
the other two are ausf D's. Such mixes of different models were very common
in operational units. [Bundesarchiv]

This ausf D is another vehicle from the 192nd Sturmgeschütz Abteilung. It was hit by a shell that smashed into the side armor above the vision block; the impact and disintegration of the projectile damaged the mudguard which has been removed, as was the 9 mm armored extension in front of the radio pannier. [Bundesarchiv]

Rear View Early StuG III

This StuG III ausf D shows yet another layout for stowing extra track across the rear of the engine section. The spare track length in turn supported much of the stowage on the engine deck. Note the trough for the folding radio antenna rod, and the cable held in the rear tow eye with a track pin.

StuG III ausf E
(SdKfz 142)

Introduced in the autumn of 1941, the StuG III ausf E represented another gradual development of the basic design. Essentially similar to the ausf D series, the ausf E featured some redesign of the superstructure. The 9 mm thick angled side plates were eliminated, leaving the 30 mm vertical sides exposed. The armored pannier for the radio on the left side was extended forward, and for use when additional radios were installed in command vehicles, a second pannier was added to the right side of the superstructure. In standard StuG III ausf E's, the second pannier was used to stow extra ammunition. The ausf E is easily identified by the short L/24 howitzer, vertical side walls, and two armored box extensions, one on each side of the superstructure.

"Dessauer," a StuG III ausf E in Russia, in the spring of 1942. The color is overall dark gray, and the markings are all in white. The rectangle is a memorial plaque dedicated to three crew members killed on 4 Sept., 1941. [Bundesarchiv]

[Right] This new StuG III ausf E shows the major change in the superstructure: the addition of the second armored box on the right side, and deletion of the 9mm angled outer side walls. Note also the revised glacis access hatches with smaller hinges; these were used on all subsequent models.

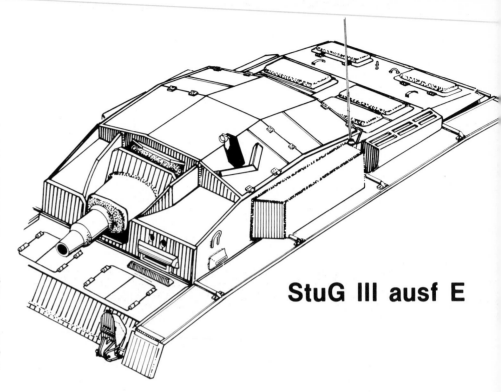

StuG III ausf E

An ausf E moving along a passage cleared through a Russian minefield in the Crimea. The mottled appearance is caused by applications of mud on the dark gray paint, along with a heavy, worn coat of dust. [Bundesarchiv]

[Above Right] Two ausf E's in the Crimea support pioneer assault troops. The vehicle on the right is a command vehicle and has just fired a round—note the barrel in full recoil, and the cloud of dust raised by the muzzle blast. This is the same vehicle shown in the minefield in the previous photo. [Bundesarchiv]

The same StuG III passing the body of a dead Russian. Mud has been used over the dark gray. Note the use of the scissors telescope in addition to the gunner's sight. This was very common, as there was no other protected vision arrangement for the commander. [Bundesarchiv]

Several StuG III's halt before an advance on Russian positions in the Crimea, June 1942. The three vehicles to the left are ausf E's; the other two are ausf D's. [Bundesarchiv]

[Below Left] A StuG III ausf E supports a pioneer assault group in the Crimean campaign, 1942. These troops were responsible for clearing mines and obstacles during an assault. [Bundesarchiv]

Snow provides the only winter camouflage on this ausf E. The crew wears heavy winter clothing, and the commander has even bandaged his nose to protect it from the cold and wind. Again, sunshade tubes are fitted to the spotting telescope, to reduce snow glare.

StuG III ausf E
(SdKfz 142)

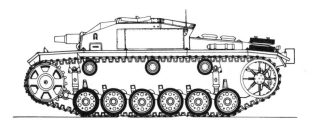

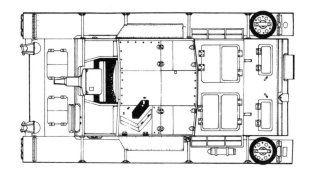

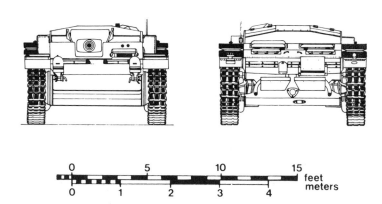

0 5 10 15 feet
0 1 2 3 4 meters

1:76 th scale (4 mm:1 foot)

A StuG III ausf E in Russia, early 1942. This shows the details of the left side stowage. Many ausf E's had the spare roadwheels stowed at the sides to leave the rear area free for bulky items, such as crates, tarpaulins, etc. This unit named its vehicles after the great cats--others were named "Leopard" and "Löwe" ["Lion"]. [Bundesarchiv]

"Leopard" shows the large amount of stowage often carried on StuG III's. This crew has been supplied with complete cold weather clothing. Note the makeshift rack and brackets for the spare track. Each unit usually made up its own pattern from scrap, and there were many variations. [Bundesarchiv]

StuG III ausf F (SdKfz 142/1)

The obvious superiority of the Russian T34/76 and KV-1 tanks came as a shock to German troops and military leaders. Poor tactics by the Russians, and somewhat limited numbers of these fine vehicles, enabled the Germans to blunt the initial Russian assaults made with the new tanks. However, time was clearly limited for the Germans to develop weapons to counter these new threats. The StuG III ausf A-E were pressed into service where necessary to fight the Russian armor. Though the L/24 howitzer was of very limited use against the T34 and KV-1, the heavy front armor of the StuG III gave the crews a much better chance to close with the Soviet armor and destroy it at close range. Nonetheless, many vehicles were destroyed before they could get close enough, and a better gun was essential.

In late 1941, Hitler ordered that more powerful weapons were to be fitted to several German armored vehicles as soon as possible. The PzKpfw III ausf J received the L/60 version of the 5 cm KwK 39, and the PzKpfw IV ausf F received the 7.5 cm KwK 40, L/43. The StuG III ausf F received a similar weapon, designated StuK 40. In the tank gun (KwK 40), the recoil cylinders were placed on each side of the barrel and breech; in the StuK 40, they were placed above the barrel, in order to provide adequate clearance for traverse within the fixed superstructure without having to enlarge the aperture for the gun.

A new welded block mantlet with 30 mm front armor was designed and the central part of the roof was raised in the rear and an electric fan and ventilator very similar to those in the PzKpfw III and IV were fitted in the raised section.

The L/43 gun vastly improved the fighting abilities of the StuG III, and kills rose sharply on the Eastern Front. Because of its low silhouette, the StuG III ausf F proved an excellent ambush weapon, and was able to knock out the T34 at long range.

After a number of StuG III ausf F's had been built with the L/43 gun, a new version was introduced. The chassis design was based on that of the PzKpfw III ausf J (8/ZW) mechanical layout, and as a result, the entire engine deck and rear hull areas were altered. The cast deck ventilators ran lengthwise rather than across the vehicle, and the tailplate was redesigned to eliminate the bolted flange joint across the upper rear piece of armor.

The gun was lengthened another 5 calibers, being designated 7.5 cm StuK 40, L/48. Additional 30 mm armor was added to the 50 mm nose plates and the driver's and offside front 50 mm plates. During ausf F production, the roof plates over the driver and the offside extension next to the gun had been raised in the rear to come up to the top of the side plates and superstructure front plate, and the F/8 also had this arrangement. Some earlier ausf F's were later retrofitted with the L/48 gun, but were otherwise unaltered. A few ausf F/8's

This front view of a column of early StuG III ausf F's shows the great resemblance to the ausf E. The basic superstructure is identical except for the raised center rear roof and the addition of the ventilator and extractor fan on this raised section.

had the L/48 guns with the older single baffle muzzle brake; others had a folding shield on the roof for an MG 34 for the loader, and some had schürzen plates fitted.

Ausf F and F/8 vehicles served primarily on the Eastern Front, where their low silhouettes and excellent armament made them effective antitank weapons. Some vehicles also saw service in Italy and in the last stages of the North African campaign in Tunisia.

With the increasing use of the StuG III as an antitank weapon, infantry units once more were left without an armored support vehicle. Therefore, a new, true assault gun was proposed in 1942. Based on the StuG III ausf F, the new vehicle mounted a modified version of the 10.5 cm le F.H. 18, the standard German light field howitzer, and was designated "Sturmhaubitze 42" (StuH 42), ausf F. It was identical to the StuG III except for the gun. The StuH 42 ausf F was built in very limited numbers because of the introduction of the following version, the ausf G; it received the model number SdKfz 142/2.

Often misidentified before, this vehicle is a standard StuG III ausf F fitted with the standard Stu K 40, L/43. The barrel has been damaged, breaking off much of the barrel and muzzle brake. When the vehicle is sent back for repairs, the gun will be replaced.

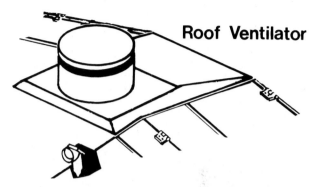

Roof Ventilator

[Below Left] This StuG III ausf F of "Grossdeutschland" was damaged by a mine. As usually happened, the mudguard has been torn badly, and will probably be removed. Markings are white and the color scheme is dark yellow lightly oversprayed with red brown. Note the trough for the antenna rod, and the strap holding the jerricans on the smoke discharger box.

Rear view of an ausf F in Russia, showing the original hull design with the bolted flanged joint between the engine section deck and the lower hull. The raised roof and ventilator show well here.

This StuG III ausf F has been fitted with the later L/48 gun. Upgrading older vehicles was a standard practice, covering armament, mechanical details, and even extra armor. [Bundesarchiv]

Another ausf F retaining the ausf E superstructure front. Again, the L/48 has been refitted, and some paint has been burned off the muzzle brake. Another type of winter clothing is shown here. [Bundesarchiv]

StuG III ausf F
(SdKfz 142/1)

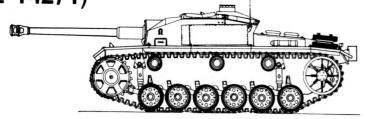

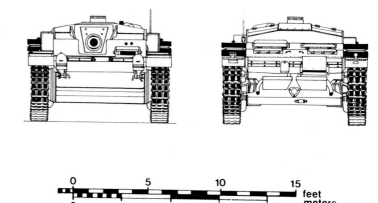

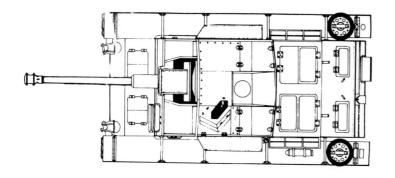

0   5   10   15

feet

0   1   2   3   4

meters

1:76 th scale (4 mm:1 foot)

Road Wheel

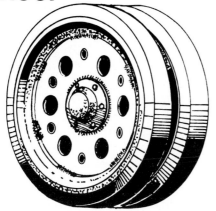

Changing a pair of roadwheels on an ausf F. This, too, was a normal part of maintenance, done whenever the wheels or tires were worn or damaged. Both these men wear the green work fatigues.

This front view of an ausf F in Russia shows details of the nose fittings of the ausf F chassis. The old style tow shackles and cover headlights were carried over from the ausf E. A very interesting detail here is that the area over the driver's roof has been filled with a layer of concrete to improve the ballistic shape and give better protection. The offside extension roof has been treated the same way.

Concrete Fill

The loader's roof hatch is shown in this detail shot of the right side of an ausf F. The spare wheel stowage is a field modification, made up by the local units from scrap. Again, concrete has been used to fill in the space above the superstructure extension next to the gun, and this would have been done to the driver's roof also.

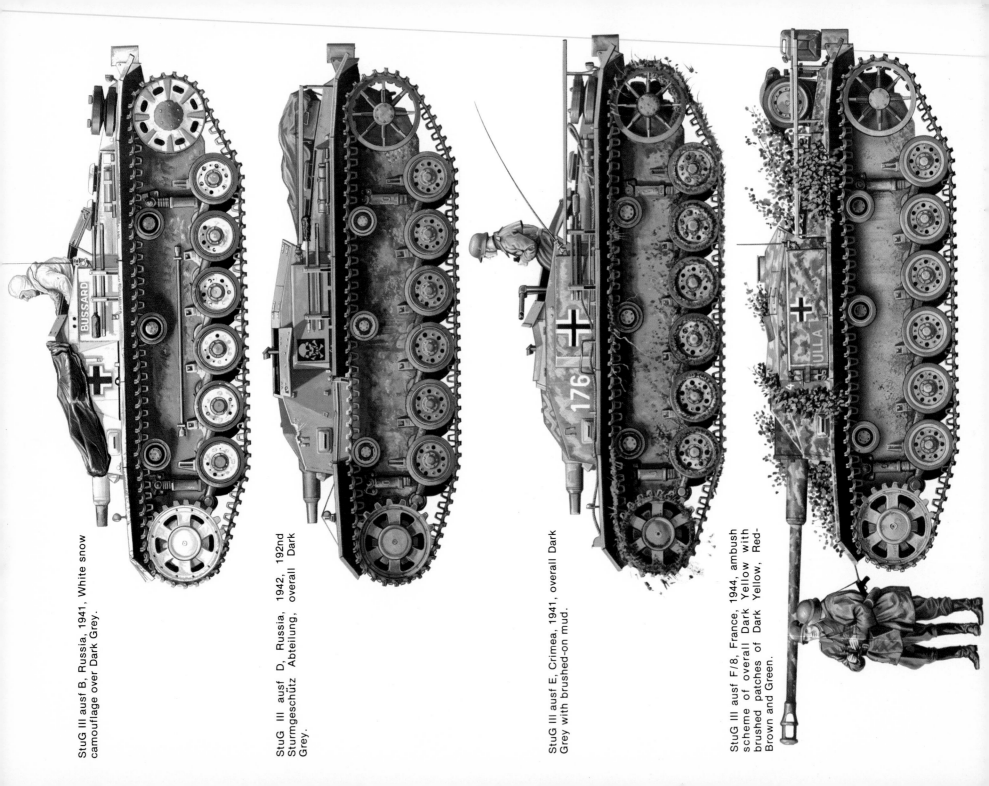

StuG III ausf B, Russia, 1941, White snow camouflage over Dark Grey.

StuG III ausf D, Russia, 1942, 192nd Sturmgeschütz Abteilung, overall Dark Grey.

StuG III ausf E, Crimea, 1941, overall Dark Grey with brushed-on mud.

StuG III ausf F/8, France, 1944, ambush scheme of overall Dark Yellow with brushed patches of Dark Yellow, Red-Brown and Green.

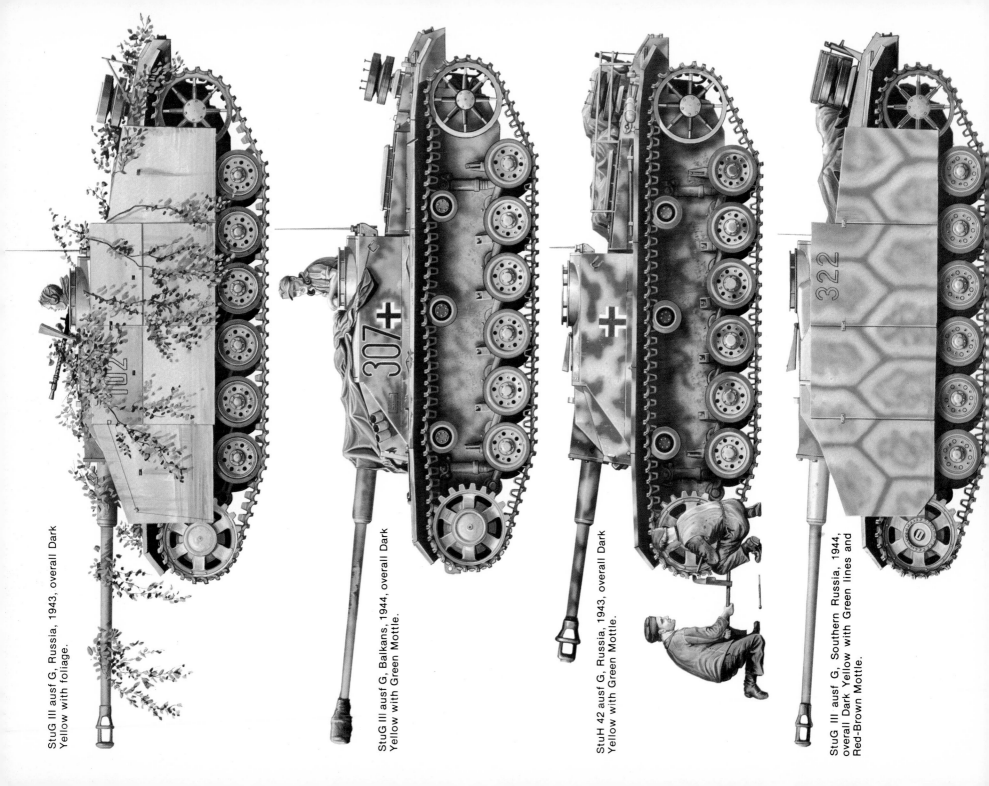

StuG III ausf G, Russia, 1943, overall Dark Yellow with foliage.

StuG III ausf G, Balkans, 1944, overall Dark Yellow with Green Mottle.

StuH 42 ausf G, Russia, 1943, overall Dark Yellow with Green Mottle.

StuG III ausf G, Southern Russia, 1944, overall Dark Yellow with Green lines and Red-Brown Mottle.

StuG III ausf F/8
(SdKfz 142/1)

Loading ammunition into a StuG III ausf F/8. Note how the roof hatch supports the shield for the loader's machine gun. This machine gun is an MG 15, a flexibly-mounted aircraft gun. Use of aircraft guns became more common later in the war; this one may have been salvaged.

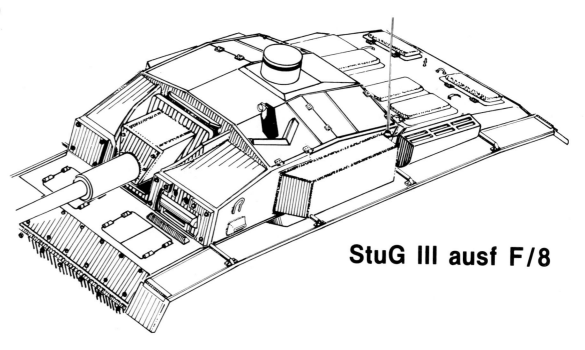

StuG III ausf F/8

Two StuG III ausf F/8's in Russia, 1943. These two vehicles are unusual in that they have the longer L/48 guns, but have the early globular single baffle muzzle brake. Note the wire guard cage over the gunner's sight on the nearer vehicle. [Bundesarchiv]

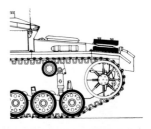

An ausf F/8 in Italy during training exercises. Here is seen the extra 30 mm armor bolted over the 50 mm basic armor, the L/48 gun, and the revised roof plates over the driver and offside extension. The mottling has been applied with brushes or sponges. Another vehicle in this unit was named "ERIKA," seen in "Panzer Colors." [Bundesarchiv]

StuG III ausf F/8

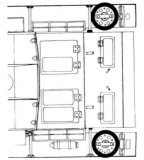

1:76 th scale (4 mm : 1 foot)

A fine study of a StuG III ausf F/8, showing the L/48 gun and the revised engine deck, based on the chassis design of the PzKpfw III ausf J. This vehicle, seen in Italy, 1943, has an unusual bracket for holding the spare track on the engine deck, and a wire cage for the sight. [Bundesarchiv]

StuG III ausf G (SdKfz 142/1)

The final production version of the StuG III series, the ausf G, appeared early in 1943. Though rather extensive, the changes introduced on the ausf G were based on the existing design of the ausf F/8. The chassis was essentially unchanged; early ausf G's had 50 mm nose armor, to which were added the extra 30 mm plates, by bolting or welding. As production got under way, 80 mm nose plates were introduced, and were used for the remainder of ausf G production.

The greatest change was in the superstructure. Months of combat experiences and many unit reports had pinpointed many weaknesses in the earlier designs and the ausf G was intended to correct many of these. The front plates were standardized at 80 mm thickness, with 30 mm plates bolted to the basic 50 mm armor; this allowed the continued use of the old driver's visor, designed for 50 mm plate. On later vehicles the 80 mm front plate to the right of the gun was one piece of 80 mm armor. Very early vehicles still had the driver's binocular vision device (fahrerfernrohr) installed and they can be identified by the two holes above the driver's visor.

The main body of the superstructure was widened to extend over the tracks, enclosing the spaces occupied by the armored radio boxes. The roof was raised in the rear and a new cupola was installed for the commander. The old flush mounted roof flaps and binocular spotting telescope had seriously limited the commander's vision from inside the vehicle. The new cupola was a cylindrical structure, on top of which were arranged 8 episcopes, each of which could be raised or lowered independently; on top of the episcopes was a ring of thin armor. The central hatch in the cupola hinged at the rear, and consisted of two sections: the main hatch and a small flap which could be opened separately to allow use of the binocular scopes without opening the main hatch. Clear plastic inserts protected the episcopes.

The ventilator and fan were mounted in the center of the rear roof plate on early vehicles, but then were moved to the vertical rear wall of the superstructure over the engine deck. The loader's split hatch opened to the front and rear. The front folding roof shield for the loader's auxiliary machine gun was standardized on the StuG III ausf G; the front loader's hatch plate had a locking hasp that engaged a hook on the shield and stabilized it during firing. An aperture was cut in the shield for the gun and a bracket was provided to hold the weapon in position. A second bracket at the top of the shield was to mount the machine gun for antiaircraft use. Most early vehicles were also equipped with smoke dischargers, 3 on each side of the superstructure. "Schürzen" antibazooka plates were introduced during production. Many vehicles did not have these fitted, as this was done by the units in the field; the

brackets and skirts had to be shipped unassembled because of railroad width clearance limitations.

The 10.5 cm howitzer-armed StuH 42 ausf G was identical to the StuG III except for the installation of the howitzer; this used the same welded block mantlet with a fatter barrel guide tube to accommodate the larger barrel of the howitzer. A double-baffle muzzle brake was fitted to the howitzer. Vehicles were taken from StuG III production for completion as StuH 42's, and these weapons began reaching service units in early 1943.

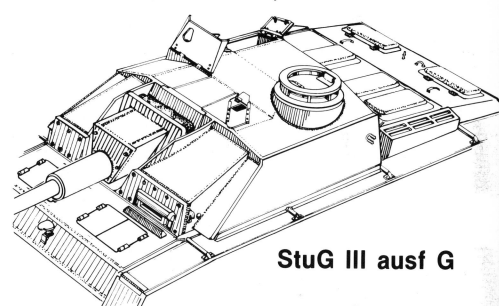

StuG III ausf G

A good view of an early StuG III ausf G in Russia, showing the bolted 30 mm additional armor. The original headlights have been replaced by the Notek light in the center of the nose. Though not visible here, this vehicle's markings include 23 black kill rings on the barrel.

The crew of "25" are washing off the winter white camouflage paint. The entire chassis has been coated with thin mud, hiding the base color completely. The front plate of the block mantlet has been replaced after maintenance but not bolted in place. [Bundesarchiv]

[Above Left] This view shows a number of interesting details of an early ausf G. In addition to the extra armor and Notek light, this vehicle carries smoke dischargers. Note the padded cushion on the cupola hatch. Skirting plates are stacked against the far side of the superstructure. [Bundesarchiv]

Seen in Russia, this early StuG III ausf G passes two burned-out late production T34/76 model 42's. Extra armor has been bolted to the nose, and this vehicle carries a second radio antenna, indicating that it is a command vehicle.

An interesting pair of vehicles--both are early ausf G's, the near example having bolted additional nose armor, the rear vehicle having the extra armor welded to the nose plates. Towing vehicles this way was not recommended--indeed it was usually prohibited--but in many cases, such actions salvaged equipment which otherwise would have been lost.

Twill Fatigue Work Suit, 1943

Another early ausf G, in northern Russia. This vehicle has the welded additional 30 mm nose armor. The small flap hanging down from the cupola hatch allowed the commander to use the binocular spotting telescope without having to open the entire cupola hatch. [Bundesarchiv]

A column of StuG III ausf G's seen in France, 1944. All are dark yellow and the muzzle covers indicate a unit moving through a rear area. Many units were sent to France for refitting or training.

[Above Left] An ausf G in Italy, 1943. This vehicle has no zimmerit or deflector casting for the cupola. There are two projectiles remaining in the smoke discharger.

Spare Road Wheel Storage

An interesting view of a command StuG III ausf G of "Grossdeutschland" in Russia. Note the two antennas and the strap steel engine deck railing. These railings were fabricated by unit ordnance workshops and varied greatly in design and construction. There are apparently ceremonial garlands around the cupola and gun barrel.

Another ausf G in Russia-- this example displays a metal pennant and a good deal of extra stowage. The wood beam across the rear has been chained to the railing through brackets bolted to the ends of the beam.

[Above Right] The crew of this ausf G wears the reversible white/camouflage suits, here with the camouflage out. The ammunition cases for the 7.5 cm StuK 40 were fatter and shorter than the PAK 40 ammunition, facilitating stowage and handling in a cramped vehicle interior. The wire strung along the skirts was used to tie foliage to the vehicle for better concealment.

[Below Right] Reloading ammunition in a StuH 42 ausf G. The second man from the right is a Russian prisoner of war, serving as an ammunition carrier. As can be seen, the 10.5 cm howitzer used separated ammunition, and several strengths of propelling charges could be used.

As this StuG III ausf G moves across a plowed field in the flat plains of southern Russia, the loader fits his MG 34 into the mounting bracket on the roof shield. T-34 tracks have been used to improve the protection on the sides.

Production Development

Because the ausf G remained in production from early 1943 to the end of the war, it was subject to more changes and modifications than any of the preceding types. In addition to the introduction of "schürzen," zimmerit antimagnetic cement was used after production had been under way. Several patterns were used in the zimmerit, probably reflecting factory variations; a common type had a "waffle plate" pattern applied with a pattern plate or roller. Also, many vehicles did not have the smoke dischargers fitted, through it is not known when they were discontinued, or even if all the production facilities used them at any time.

The original cupola projected from the roof side plates, and presented a useful target, as the armor was only 30 mm thick. Therefore a cast armor shield was welded to the roof and front of the cupola to deflect shells and bullets up or to the side. Improvements were made in the schürzen installation, including cutting away the lower front corners to minimize snagging the skirts on obstacles, and adoption of loosely hung skirting instead of the fastened type on earlier vehicles. In 1944, a new mantlet was introduced for the StuG III ausf G. Comprising a one-piece rounded casting, it was referred to as "Saukopfblende" ("boar's head" mount). The cast "Saukopf" was intended to replace the built up block mantlet, though a number of vehicles with late production details still retained the block mantlet. The rubber-tire return rollers were replaced by all-steel rollers to conserve rubber.

The StuH 42 also received the cast "Saukopf" mantlet; of necessity, this was much larger than the one for the StuG III, but was similar in shape; at this time the muzzle brake was still installed. The "Saukopf" installation was used on only some of the StuH 42's; it never replaced the box mantlet, and both types were built to the end of production. Late StuH 42's with the block mantlet received coaxial machine guns which fired through the front plate of the mantlet--this new weapon gave the crews a much better defense against infantry. The muzzle brake was usually left off the later vehicles, without serious problems.

Both StuG III and StuH 42 vehicles received a further modification to the superstructure. The loader's roof hatches were turned 90° so they opened to the sides, and a remote controlled mount for an external machine gun was placed in the roof ahead of the hatch. The outside hatch door could be held open to protect the gunner as he reloaded the roof MG. An angled shield protected the machine gun and ammo drum from fragments or small arms fire. At the same time, to improve the defense against infantry, a "close-in defense weapon" ("Nahverteidigungswaffe"), identical to that fitted in "Panther" and "Tiger" tanks, was placed in the right front part of the roof. This weapon rotated 360° and could protect all sides of the vehicle. StuG III's with the block mantlet also had the coaxial machine gun, and some very late vehicles had a coaxial gun in the "Saukopf" mantlet for the 7.5 cm StuK 40. Zimmerit was largely discontinued by the early part of 1945; thus, some late vehicles had it and others didn't. A British technical report mentions a fixed cupola on two captured specimens, but the extent of use is not known. It is likely that there were variations among vehicles built at different factories, resulting from availability of different components.

An ausf G in the Caucasus, 1943. The crew members wear a variety of uniforms, including the field gray assault gun uniform, green tropical uniform, and rush green denim fatigue suit. Many variations in mixing parts of uniforms were seen in combat units. On the upper nose plate—which carries an untextured coating of zimmerit—is a memorial cross for a dead crewman and a tactical sign.

An ausf G being driven off a flatcar, showing a common way of attaching foliage to a vehicle. Merely hooking the inverted branches over the upper edge of the skirting was sufficient to hold them in place—until the vehicle went through heavy brush or undergrowth. [Bundesarchiv]

There were many variations in the zimmerit patterns applied to StuG III's—even to the point of a smooth coat of zimmerit without texturing. Here are three patterns that were used. The upper left vehicle has a hand-raked pattern of lines, in this case applied over a previous dimpled pressed pattern. The lower left StuG III has a hand-troweled pattern very similar to that used on PzKpfw IV's. The vehicle above has the "waffle plate" design applied with a metal plate or roller, and most often found on later vehicles with "saukopf" cast mantlets.

Zimmerit

StuG III ausf G

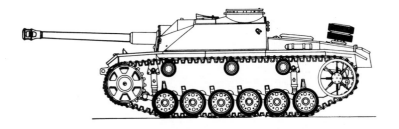

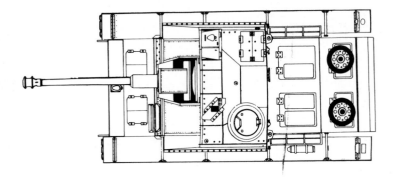

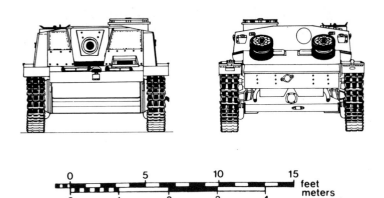

0 5 10 15 feet
0 1 2 3 4 meters

1:76 th scale (4 mm:1 foot)

Two views of a slightly later production StuG III ausf G. The nose armor is 80 mm base, and the raked zimmerit pattern is used. The camouflage paint was applied with a sponge. Hungarian infantry ride on these German vehicles during the campaign in southern Russia. Note the "C" tow hooks hung in the front two shackle holes.

A close up of the loader and folding 10 mm armor shield for the roof MG 34. The latch on the front hatch segment slipped over a hook on the shield, bracing the whole structure. The mounting bracket at the top of the shield was to mount the gun for antiaircraft fire.

[Left, Above & Below] Two ways to fire the loader's roof machine gun—the better protected way was from inside the vehicle as shown above; this gunner fires an MG 42, bouncing empty cases off the roof hatch. The man in the lower picture is on the engine deck, completely unprotected from the sides or rear. Many crewmen used these weapons outside the vehicles.

Two StuG III ausf G's in Italy, 1944. Both vehicles carry large fuel drums and the "waffle plate" zimmerit coating. The men on the vehicles are infantry and StuG III crewmen.

[Above Left] The track tension adjusting mechanism shows clearly on this ausf G being transported to a repair area in Italy, 1943. The crewmen wear the later low ankle boots—with the more usual long trousers, these were usually worn with buckled ankle cuffs, though many assault gun troops simply bloused the trousers directly into these low boots.

This StuG III ausf G of the 244th Sturmgeschütz Brigade is being refuelled from an Opel "Maultier" halftrack truck. The soldier sitting on the fuel drum is working a hand-operated "wobble" pump to transfer fuel to the vehicle. Note the folding steps on the dropped rear gate of the truck; the one on the right is folded up. A good view of the fuel transfer pump, carried on a Panther, may be seen on p. 62 of "Panzer Colors." [Bundesarchiv]

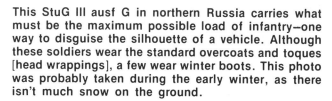

This StuG III ausf G in northern Russia carries what must be the maximum possible load of infantry—one way to disguise the silhouette of a vehicle. Although these soldiers wear the standard overcoats and toques [head wrappings], a few wear winter boots. This photo was probably taken during the early winter, as there isn't much snow on the ground.

[Below Left] A snow-camouflaged ausf G passes through a burning Russian village. The commander wears a winter fur-lined cap and reversible white suit. The other side of the suit was overall field gray or a camouflage pattern.

Sturmgeschütz units were often engaged in the heaviest fighting, and award for bravery and service were common. This much-decorated crewman has been awarded the Knights Cross, 1st and 2nd class Iron Crosses, Assault badge, and a Wound badge. Although the Germans didn't name their vehicles as often as U.S. and British troops, names were used. [Bundesarchiv]

Ausf G interiors

The interior of an ausf G, showing some roof detail and the binocular telescope mounted in the cupola. This was the standard artillery spotting scope and could be used on the folding tripod, or on a variety of brackets provided with many vehicles. Again, note the cupola episcopes seen here.

[Below Right] Loading a modern gun requires care to avoid injury. The loader uses his fist to ram home the casing, reducing the chances of getting his hand or fingers caught. The rising breechblock will knock his hand up through the top of the breech as it snaps closed.

The commander of a StuG III ausf G talks to his gunner. Some of the cupola details can be seen; the padded leather ring cushion around the hatch opening, the mounting bracket for the binocular telescope often used for detailed observations, and the episcopes around the cupola periphery--these were raised or lowered individually as needed.

Two loader/radio operators in StuG III command vehicles. The man on the right wears a reversible white/camouflage uniform. The other loader has to contend with extra ammo piled in front of his extra radio equipment. In most

StuG III ausf G's, radios were carried only on the left below the cupola and were intended for the vehicle commander. Command and observation vehicles had extra radios on the right side wall, as shown here.

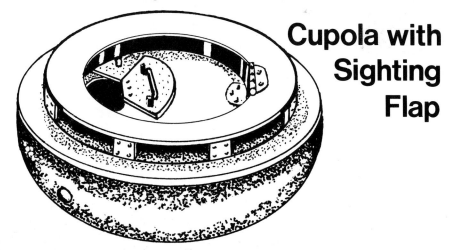

Cupola with Sighting Flap

The interior of an ausf G cupola, showing the padded ring cushions, inner cover for the ring of episcopes, and the commander's binocular spotting telescope.

[Left Top, Middle & Bottom] This damaged StuG III ausf G of the 259th Sturmgeschütz Brigade is being rebuilt at an outside repair facility. It was hit on the right side near the roof, which has been unbolted and removed to allow replacement of the gun and other equipment. Here the new gun and pedestal mount are being lowered into the vehicle. After the gun pedestal is bolted to the floor, the roof will be replaced. The crane is mounted on a Bussing-NAG 4.5 tonne truck.

[Above Center] Here the same truck lifts the engine into place on another 259th StuG Brigade vehicle. The unit sign has been painted on the rear plate in black and white.

[Above Right] The joys of physical fitness are demonstrated by this crewman as he cranks up the starter for the Maybach HL120TRM engine. In cold weather, this was a two-man job, and below freezing, the engine often had to be preheated before it would start.

Under cover of a smoke screen, StuG III's and APC's advance during the campaign in southern Russia in the summer of 1943. The StuG III's are ausf G's and the APC's are the late pattern SdKfz 250 1-tonne halftracks. [Bundesarchiv]

[Below Left] A late StuG III ausf G with an interesting detail—it carries the rounded layer of concrete over the superstructure front but retains the older welded block mantlet and folding roof machine gun shield. Note the chassis number painted on the "Hummel."

An ausf G in Russia, 1943. This example has a raked pattern in the zimmerit and carries the cast deflector for the cupola. This is a command vehicle.

"Saukopf" mantlet:

A Sturmgeschütz unit moves up to the front lines in central Russia, 1944. This unit uses a 3-digit numbering system on the vehicles—the nearest one is "111". All of the "saukopf" cast mantlets have been painted with cartoon features, in black and white, to resemble boars. [Bundesarchiv]

A late production StuG III ausf G with the cast "saukopf" mantlet and later type of skirt installation, in which the "schürzen" were hung loosely from teeth on the rails so they would not tear off the brackets if they snagged on an obstruction. Note the dirty, chipped coat of zimmerit.

A later production ausf G with "saukopf" mantlet. Note the distinctive "waffle iron" pattern in the zimmerit, usually seen on these later vehicles. Color is overall dark yellow.

Another later ausf G in France. It is dark yellow with dark green patches. As was rather common with StuG III's, the gun barrel is darker than the rest of the vehicle, perhaps as a result of heat from extended firing.

Loading ammunition into an ausf G in Italy. As can be seen, shells were loaded through all the access hatches, depending where they were to be stowed. Many vehicles carried as much ammunition as the crews could stack inside the fighting compartment.

This top view of a late ausf G shows the cupola episcope ring, cast cupola shield, and the bolted mounting for the "schürzen" bracket on the superstructure. Note the canvas dust cover on the gun mantlet, and the smooth spot in the zimmerit—for the railroad class shipping label.

This ausf G has a "saukopf" mantlet hidden under the passengers, and belongs to an SS unit on the Russian front. Remnants of a white camouflage scheme may be seen on the mantlet and side skirts. The SS infantry are wearing reversible camouflage suits, low boots and ankle cuffs.

[Below Left] A column of StuG III ausf G's in Italy, 1944. Note the chipped zimmerit and incomplete brackets for the side skirts. All the crewmen wear the field gray assault gun uniforms.

Oberltw. Alfred Müller of StuG Brig. 901 discusses map references with his men. Müller's StuG III has the "saukopf" mantlet and "waffle plate" zimmerit under all the foliage. The 16 kill rings on the barrel are in white. Müller wears the Knight's Cross at his throat.

Late production ausf G

StuG III ausf G

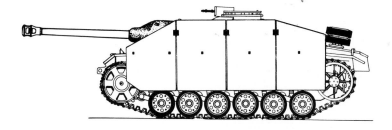

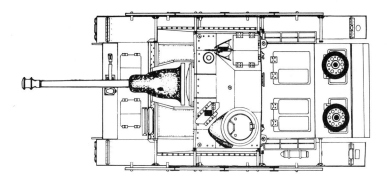

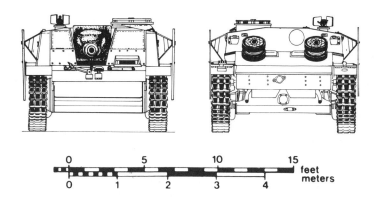

0   5   10   15 feet
0   1   2   3   4 meters

1:76 th scale (4 mm:1 foot)

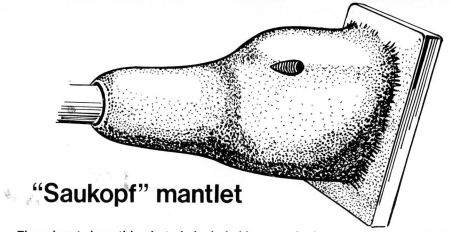

"Saukopf" mantlet

Though not clear, this photo is included because it shows an unusual vehicle. This StuH 42 has a large "saukopf" mantlet and an unusual gun travel lock on the glacis plate. Also, a layer of concrete has been added to the side front plates but not to the driver's roof or extension roof. The cast cupola shield is shown well here. Compare with a similar vehicle on p. 82 of "Panzer Colors."

American infantry inspect a knocked-out late StuG III ausf G. This vehicle retains the welded block mantlet, but carries a coaxial machine gun—the muzzle opening is just below the upper right bolt. The weapon in the remote-controlled roof mg mount is missing. Note the lack of zimmerit. The gun travel lock was released by elevating the barrel—a spring attached to the chain pulled the lock out of the way and cleared the gun for action without requiring any of the crewmen to leave the vehicle. The Notek light is just next to the travel lock. [U.S. Army]

Remote Control MG 34

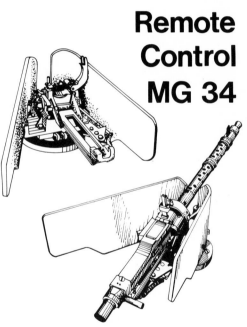

This close view of a burned-out ausf G shows how the side-opening loader's hatch shielded the loader as he reloaded the remote-control MG 34. Again, this vehicle retains the welded block mantlet, with a coaxial mg. The skirting on this vehicle is a different design, bolted directly to mudguard brackets, and being cut much lower. Spare track sections were held in the brackets on the superstructure side. [Archives Publiques]

This captured late StuG III ausf G, being used by troops of the U.S. 104th Infantry Division, represents the final production type. Not many StuG III's received the layer of concrete as shown here. Note the "schürzen" brackets on the mudguard and the gun travel lock and base for the Notek "tarnscheinwerfer." An interesting variation is the use of an MP 44 assault rifle in the remote control mg mount in place of the usual MG 34. [U.S. Army]

Aircraft   Armor   Weapons   Warships

squadron/signal publications

IN ACTION